F|

M000296328

WILD SWIMMING
A brief and benighted history

BY
MAREK HORN

From an original idea conceived of and developed
by Marek Horn and Julia Head

WILD SWIMMING

A FullRogue Production

Commissioned with support from Bristol Old Vic Ferment.

Supported by Pleasance Futures.

Wild Swimming was first performed at Pleasance Beneath, Edinburgh, in August 2019 as part of the Edinburgh Festival Fringe. It then opened at the Weston Studio, Bristol Old Vic, in September 2019. The original cast and creative team were as follows:

Oscar	Annabel Baldwin
Nell	Alice Lamb
Writer	Marek Horn
Director	Julia Head
Designer	Zoe Brennan
Producers	Ruby Gilmour
	Joseff Harris
Stage Manager	Hannah Clare

With thanks to Jason King and Joseff Harris for their support in lighting and sound and to Beth Folan and Marianne Barrouillet for their technical support.

BIOGRAPHIES

Annabel Baldwin | Oscar

Annabel is an actor and theatre-maker from London. She trained at ArtsEd. Her theatre credits include *Harry Potter and the Cursed Child*, where she played Moaning Myrtle in the original company and then Delphi Diggory (Palace Theatre). Other credits include *The Wolves* (Theatre Royal Stratford East), *Scripted* (Sheffield Crucible), *Dear Elizabeth* (The Gate), *The Jewish Enquirer* (TV credit).

Alice Lamb | Nell

Alice is an actor and theatre-maker from Bristol. She trained at Manchester School of Theatre. Her acting credits include *Goldilock Stock and the Three Smoking Bears* (Wardrobe Theatre/Theatre Royal Plymouth), *Autobiographer* (Melanie Wilson & Fuel). She is the co-creator of *Mental* by Kane Power Theatre, which won the first Mental Health Award at the Edinburgh Fringe. She is a cast member of the world's longest-running improvised narrative *Closer Each Day: The Improvised Soap Opera* (Wardrobe Theatre).

Marek Horn | Writer

Marek is a Writer on Attachment at the Bristol Old Vic as part of their Open Session scheme. In 2017 he was shortlisted for Out of Joint's WiT Award for his play *Yeager, Conrad, Grissom, Glenn*. His plays *Further. Still* and *A Short Lecture on the Spiritual Relevance and Potential Utility of the Bhagavad Gita in the Nuclear Age* have had staged readings at the Old Red Lion in Islington. His play *Yellowfin* was given a rehearsed reading at the same venue.

Julia Head | Director

Julia is a director from Bristol. In 2018 she received a Bristol Old Vic Ferment Leverhulme Arts Scholarship. She works extensively with Bristol Old Vic's Engagement department and was awarded the Henry Augustine Forse Award for her contribution to Engagement. She is an Associate Director of Ad Infinitum, Twisted Theatre and Headlong Futures. Julia is also a trustee of MAYK.

Zoë Brennan | Designer

Zoë is a designer of live performance. She has recently graduated from the Royal Welsh College of Music and Drama with a degree in Design for Performance. She was part of the National Theatre Design development weekend in 2016. Designs include *The Master and Margarita* (ZOO Venues Ed Fringe Festival) and *Spring Awakening* (Caird Studio). Scenic art experience includes *Punk Rock* (Bute Theatre) and *The Crystal Maze* (RDF Productions).

Ruby Gilmour | Producer

Ruby is a producer based in Bristol. She has recently graduated from Bristol University with a degree in Theatre and Performance Studies. She has worked within the Bristol Old Vic's Producing and Programming department and is currently part of the Papatango WriteWest producer's scheme.

Joseff Harris | Producer

Joseff is a producer from Bristol. He was the Co-Artistic Director of Sofar Sounds Bristol and was responsible for relaunching the company in 2016. Sofar Sounds is dedicated to making live music more accessible, intimate and absorbing. He also worked with Bristol Old Vic's Engagement department to produce the 2019 NT Connections Festival.

Hannah Clare | Stage Manager

Hannah is a stage manager and wardrobe assistant based in Bristol. She is a graduate of the Bristol Old Vic Theatre School. Her credits include Assistant Stage Manager on *Touching The Void* (National Tour), Wigs Manager on *A Christmas Carol* (Bristol Old Vic), Wardrobe Manager *Hair the Musical* (Vaults, London), Stage Manager on *Ferment Fortnight Season* (Bristol Old Vic).

SUPPORTED BY

Bristol Old Vic Ferment

Bristol Ferment is Bristol Old Vic's artist development programme. We work with artists and companies in a variety of ways to support and develop their work and practice. Ferment has been running for over 9 years. In that time we have developed a number of artists to make work here in the South West that has toured nationally and internationally.

We support artists through 2 routes:

The Forum, a free and simple to join artist network for any artist in the South West that offers a range of development opportunities and benefits to engage with Bristol Old Vic and other artists in the forum.

Supported Artists & Companies, individual artists or groups that Ferment invests in to develop work with us, or to develop their practice across scales.

bristololdvic.org.uk/ferment

Pleasance Futures

Pleasance Futures is at the very heart of the Pleasance. For over 30 years we have provided a valuable platform and launch pad for a huge collection of artists, both at the Edinburgh Festival Fringe and Pleasance Islington.

We recognise how important it is to help open the door for talent, creating opportunities, supporting ambition and encouraging excellence. Our key charitable aims are to foster innovation in performance and to offer valuable artistic opportunities to young creatives. We call this wealth of artist development and support Pleasance Futures.

pleasance.co.uk/futures

FULLROGUE

FullRogue are a theatre company from Bristol.

We are interested in two things:

- The development of new theatre texts
- **Jeopardising** and potentially **destroying** said texts

We exist to *stress test** new plays *in* live performance in order to explore and CELEBRATE the fragility *of* live performance.

Plays aren't sacred, control over the theatrical event is an illusion. We always want the text, the actors, the set and the costume to be working to breaking point. We treat new plays with the confidence that they are indestructible... they may not be.

FullRogue are an associate company of Bristol Ferment. *Wild Swimming* is our first show.

Alice Lamb and Annabel Baldwin in *Wild Swimming*. Design Zoë Brennan. Photo by TheOtherRichard.

Director **Julia Head**
Writer **Marek Horn**
Creative Producer **Ruby Gilmour**

Fullroguetheatre.com
🐦 @fullrogue
📷 @fulroguetheatre

* Stress test: *A form of deliberately intense testing used to determine the stability of a given system.*

DIRECTOR'S NOTE

Love. Generosity. Mischief.

I was having a conversation with my mate Jack on a night out about three years ago. We chatted for a very long time because we were drunk. Eventually he said, 'Sometimes, Julia, I wish I was born in the Victorian times, because I think I would have been more successful then.'

Ever since that conversation I wanted to make a play about men. And feminism. And Masculinity. And I wanted a man to write it. I wanted *the* MAN to write it. And I wanted this man to have to DEFEND ALL MEN, at once, in one play. Mainly because I then wanted to get really angry, destroy some stuff, and shout loudly at him.

So I approached Marek. He is our tame playwright now, but at the time he was probably the most arrogant man I had ever met. I told him my idea.

He hated the idea.

Then I told him that the show would be only a partial construction of his play – that it would be about deconstructing and potentially DESTROYING his play, live, onstage. He hated this even more. But, I convinced him to come into a rehearsal room and see what I meant. It was full of costumes and crisps and Nerf guns and he hated it so much it made him a bit sick in his mouth.

And then he realised that he was actually terrified, and that being terrified might actually be good, and out of this tension FullRogue was formed.

We believe there are always two plays being performed. One is the play *Wild Swimming* by Marek Horn, and the other is two actors attempting to perform the play *Wild Swimming* and ultimately failing. These two worlds should be constantly present and not always in agreement. With this comes the agency of an actor. We believe every actor to have just as much creative agency as anyone else. They just have to make their decisions live, onstage, in front of a paying audience.

With all this in mind, there are a few things that might be useful to know about the original production:

· Both Oscar and Nell were played by women. It became apparent to us that, when a man played Oscar, Marek's voice became too loud, too important. Marek started winning, and Marek should never be allowed to win.

- There were lots of snacks and toys and props and random miscellaneous objects in the space at all times. These could be used / eaten / thrown by the actors if they ever felt the need.

- Marek's lines sound best when spoken quickly and with moderate disdain. The moment they are given the space and weight they deserve it sounds terrible and takes ages.

- We were fortunate enough to work with two fiercely talented actors, Alice and Annabel, who (of their own accord) started adding lines. Breaking out of the play to address a late audience member, commenting on the loud stomping coming from the room above, redoing bits of the scene that went wrong – both performed the play to the best of their ability, and yet were also constantly alive to the distractions of the space.

Take what is useful, abandon anything that's not. Don't feel the need to sabotage anything unless it feels irresistible.

FullRogue exists to celebrate the fragility of live performance, therefore to try and translate anything we make into a written document would be too difficult – we would need 100 copies, all dated from the specific night, all with slight variation from each other. Maybe one day when we're rich we'll do that, but for now we just have one copy.

So, those of you who saw the original production will be able to tell the world what actually happened, the night you saw it, where that thing happened and they did that special bit. And for those of you that didn't see it but are reading it now, you will be able to imagine what might have happened. What mischief we might have got up to. For it is our belief that plays should only really exist in the memory and imagination of the audience.

So read this play that Marek has written.

Value it.

Then read it all over again knowing that I tried my best to sabotage it.

Know that it survived.

And then run with it. Run fearlessly, with energy and force and with the confidence that it won't break. That these characters and the world they inhabit will come through stronger and more vibrant for having met the challenge. Believe it to be indestructible. And know that to fail can sometimes be totally glorious.

Go Boldly.

Julia Head, September 2019

WILD SWIMMING

A Brief and Benighted History

Marek Horn

For Carol, who taught me about plays
And Julia, who taught me how to play

Acknowledgements

Thank you to Nell O'Hara, Oscar Adams, James Kent, Tom Davies, Will Kelly, Lauren O'Leary, Lewis Coster, Euan Shanahan and Georgia Frost for their work on the early versions of this play; to Alice Lamb and Annabel Baldwin – two of the bravest, sharpest, silliest people I have ever had the good fortune to meet – for their gorgeous work in the show; to Joseff Harris and Ruby Gilmour for their tireless and selfless work producing the show; to Zoe Brennan for her wonderful design; to Ed Madden, Stuart Nunn, Sam Steiner and Miriam Battye for taking an exhaustive interest in my work when nobody else did; to all at Bristol Old Vic, but especially James Peries and Lucy Hunt for their early advocacy and to Ben Atterbury who has been an unerring advocate, confidante, hype-man and friend to FullRogue from the moment he arrived at the theatre.

Thank you also to my family, with a rare and special shout-out to my amazing dad. He gets a lot of shit from the rest of us, but he has done nothing but love and support us, to the very best of his ability, for nearly twenty-eight years. He is, very quietly, a total fucking hero.

And finally thank you to Julia, without whom none of this would ever have happened.

M.H., September 2019

Whoever masters form masters time

Glyn Maxwell

We are only just starting to be able to make
eye contact with the male gaze, and not just
call it reality

Lucy Prebble, Twitter, 17/11/2017

4

The Cast

NELL, *an ageless, time-travelling water sprite / a poet / a genius*

OSCAR, *an ageless, time-travelling water sprite / an aspiring poet / Nell's neighbour*

The Text

A line marked with (—) denotes that the speaker of the line is unascribed. A new (—) does not mean that the speaker *must* change, only that they may. All must be spoken and in the order as given. Both actors must learn them all and learn to play with them. A (—) represents a complete and single thought. Thoughts must not be split between actors

A 'Pause' or a 'Beat' denotes a break in the rhythm of discourse. A Beat is a short and rhythmic Pause. A 'Silence', however short, suggests the absence of the desire to speak

When Beats, Pauses and Silences are absent, this is a quick play. Play the shape of an individual thought but don't labour it. Trust the rhythm. Otherwise we'll be here all day. The text does not prescribe when characters should interrupt each other, but they *really* should

The Space

This play is made of SCENES and BREAKS OF PLAY. It is important to note that SCENES and BREAKS OF PLAY interact differently with The Space

SCENES

Have care. Show respect. Remain contained

Within the playing space there is another space – a space-within-a-space. The space is clearly marked. The **Scenes** happen here and only here. This space-within-a-space is important. Maybe it is sacred. Think about entrances and exits, about ritual, dance and magic

BREAKS OF PLAY

Have fun. Show love. Break the rules

Outside of this space-within-a-space, but within the playing space, should be the following:

– Water

– The various period-specific costumes required for the play

– Snacks

These things should probably be visible, their use anticipated by the audience. All of these things are to be utilised for the **Breaks of Play**. These **Breaks of Play** occur everywhere – the playing space, the space-within-the-space, the personal space of the audience, the auditorium as a whole. These **Breaks of Play** are playful and difficult. Think about playfulness, and the importance of competition. Think about difficulty, and the importance of collaboration

Prologue

Historically appropriate music plays. OSCAR *and* NELL *stand in tableau. They wear the clothes of the Renaissance. The lighting is low, the colours deep. Everything is static and stultifying. It's faintly, deceptively dull. But something is off. Do they wear sunglasses? Is one of them eating?*

—   We begin our poor play in the late sixteenth
        century

—   Or perhaps 'tis the early *seventeenth* century

—   Time is elastic in the theatre
        And for all such possibilities
        Our little 'O' encompasseth them all

—   Our stage
        These light pine boards

—   Think of it!

—   A deserted beach in Dorset

—   Civilisation to the east. Wilderness to the west

—   Civilisation and wilderness, together
        In tandem

—   In tension

—   And into the mix
        As if on cue
        The hero of our story

—   Oscar

—   Oscar… is back

—   Thank the stars!

—   He's just completed his first year of university
He's an heroic scholar-poet in the making

—   And our play opens as early summer blooms and
bursts into life

—   Heralding his auspicious return

—   His glorious return to the beautiful land of his
forefathers

—   His ancient family seat

Beat

—   And then there's Nell

Beat

—   Nell…
Well…
Nell isn't back

—   Because

—   Because…

—   Because, well, to put it simply, Nell never went
away

—   Nell is, what you might call, on a
'*Gap*'
'*Yah*'

—   And that's basically because…

—   Well, that's basically because…

—   That's basically because, until you were married
in Elizabethan England

—   If you were a '*Rich*' '*Bitch*' like her

—   Basically your whole fucking life was a
'*Gap*' '*Yah*'

They laugh, heartily

—   But anyway

—   Anyway

—   Anyway, it's a fine, fresh summer morning in
     Renaissance England

—   Good Queen Bess is on her throne and God is in
     Her heaven

—   And Oscar
     Has been out
     For a swim

One – A Break of Play

Chaos
There is chaos now
There is loud music[1]
There is shouting
There is running
There is a game being played

There are snacks – energy! Take on energy! Calories! Additives!
This whole thing is an additive
It's Monster Munch and Pepsi Max
You CRAVE something substantial
You want an apple but you can't have one
You bite an apple but the apple's made of SHERBET

Quick! The song is going to END
Quick! The scene is going to START

OSCAR*! Get naked*
OSCAR*! Get wet*[2]
OSCAR*! Ignore* NELL
NELL*! Ignore* OSCAR
NELL*! Eat snacks*
Be cool NELL
Be cool
NELL *you look so fucking cool I could eat you*
I could EAT you NELL*!*
I could EAT YOUR WHOLE VIBE
YOU are an apple made of SHERBET

1. The Song of the Play was meant to be 'Shakespeare's Sister' by The Smiths, but then Morrissey came out for Brexit. Julia (the director) felt that the relentless energy of 'Sur La Planche' by La Femme was right for us. She was correct.
2. In the original production this was achieved by turning the front row of the audience into 'the ocean', arming them with a variety of water-firing tools and toys – water pistols, atomisers and weed sprayers all featured.

Two – A Scene

Bright cold sunshine, waves crashing, seagulls crying

OSCAR *enters. He is naked or 'Naked'(?) and cold, certainly cold. He's been swimming. He's exhausted, half-drowned? He heads towards his clothes where he collapses to the ground, eyes closed against the glare of the sun, focusing on his breathing.* NELL *enters unseen. She stands over him. Silence*

NELL   Hello Oscar

OSCAR   *Jesus Christ*

OSCAR *scrabbles up, covering himself with his towel*

NELL   Oh, don't get up on my account

OSCAR   Where the fuck did you come from!?

NELL   I came from my house Oscar, where I live

OSCAR   *Fucking hell*

NELL   The more important question is *where did you come from?*

OSCAR   Do you mind?

It takes a second for NELL *to catch his drift*

NELL   Oh sure, yeah
Go ahead

NELL *turns around*

…Slip into some tights or something

OSCAR *starts to change. Pause*

OSCAR   How long were you stood there for?

NELL	Long enough
OSCAR	Why didn't you say anything?
NELL	I wouldn't worry too much Oscar It's nothing I haven't seen before
OSCAR	That was a long time ago, and it was different
NELL	Well it wasn't that long ago was it? And why was it different, exactly? Because it was dark? Because you'd had too much mead?
OSCAR	Something like that
NELL	Listen Oscar, In the bright morning light your penis remains as unintimidating as ever it did I'm sorry to say it but I remain completely unscandalised
OSCAR	Well that makes one of us
NELL	Oh yeah?
OSCAR	Yeah! I'm getting PTSD just thinking about it
NELL	Oh are you?
OSCAR	Yeah, I am
NELL	Well I don't remember any complaints at the time In fact I distinctly recall a *very enjoyable* eleven seconds for all involved
OSCAR	It wasn't eleven seconds
NELL	No?
OSCAR	No, it only felt like that because you were having so much fun
NELL	Ah yes, come to think of it, it *must've* been longer Because I managed to compose an entire shopping list in my head

OSCAR	That's good, Nell That's a funny joke
NELL	Thank you
OSCAR	Yeah, the idea of *you* going shopping... The idea of you getting off of your arse and doing anything at all, for yourself, really is rather fucking funny Nell, well done
NELL	You prick
OSCAR	You started it

Pause

NELL	So, I don't see you in months and then suddenly you appear, staggering out of the ocean What's going on?
OSCAR	I've been at uni You know this
NELL	I know I know this, but indulge me, Oscar
OSCAR	All I have ever done, Nell, is indulge you
NELL	Look, I'm trying to affect an air of nonchalance over here I'm trying to pretend I haven't missed you
OSCAR	Right Well, it's going really well
NELL	Yeah?
OSCAR	Yeah, That bit where you stood silently over my naked body for an extended period of time...
NELL	Yeah, alright
OSCAR	Really gave me a good impression as to how completely disinterested you are
NELL	Well what can I say? I don't see enough of you and then *suddenly* I'm

seeing *all of you*
How am I supposed to react?

Beat

Can I turn around yet?

He considers himself

OSCAR   Um… Yes, alright

NELL   Finally

She does so

Although I guess you've got to be careful
I can't imagine sand in a codpiece being very
pleasant

Beat

I could see you from the headland, you know?
I thought you were some random naked mentalist,
you're supposed to be a gentleman, Oscar

OSCAR   It's how the Greeks did it

NELL   Yeah, well you're English
English gentlemen don't swim
Certainly not… 'tackle out'

OSCAR   How *is* your Greek coming along?

NELL   It isn't
I only ever learnt what I scrounged off you

OSCAR   You were good at it

NELL   Too much Greek overheats the brain apparently,
Damages fertility or something
I don't know
Same old shit

OSCAR   How's life otherwise?

NELL   Dull
If I had it my way I'd be in London or something

OSCAR   No you wouldn't
         London's just about money these days

NELL   If you say so

         Beat

OSCAR   They'll be marrying you off soon
         That'll make a change

NELL   Don't

OSCAR   Anything underway on that front?

NELL   No
         I think they must be waiting for you to graduate
         See if anything happens there

OSCAR   Right

NELL   Not that I find the prospect particularly exciting, in
         the stark light of day

         She holds her little finger up and waggles it

OSCAR   Fuck off. It was cold

NELL   Sure

         Beat

OSCAR   I might have to disappoint you on that front
         actually

NELL   Yeah,
         That's what I'm saying

         She wiggles her finger again

OSCAR   Not because of that!

         He throws the towel over her head

NELL   Oscar, that's gross!
         That's had your dick in it

OSCAR   So?
         So have you

NELL   Okay, look we're not going to mention that ever
         again
         Okay?
         My gag reflex can't take it

OSCAR   I don't plan on coming back, is what I meant
         Not permanently, anyway

NELL   What?
         Not ever?

OSCAR   No

NELL   …Never ever!?

OSCAR   Not necessarily, no

NELL   Right
         Sounds ominous

OSCAR   Not really
         I want to travel, is all
         I've been reading about this guy, at uni, Philip
         Sidney
         Like a sort of diplomat-cum-politician-cum-
         soldier-cum-poet,
         You say English gentlemen don't swim, Nell, but
         Philip Sidney swims
         Famous for it

NELL   *Right*
         Hence…

         She gestures towards the water

OSCAR   All great men swim, Nell

NELL   *All great men swim*

OSCAR   It's a theory I'm working on

NELL   Right

OSCAR   I've been doing some reading and I think I might
         be able to spin it into my final thesis

NELL   You've only been there a year!

OSCAR   Yeah I know, but I wanna hit the ground running

NELL   I'm impressed
         Your gumption impresses me Oscar

         Pause

         Okay, how does this sound?
         You can pootle off on your Philip Sidney Tribute
         Act, Round-the-world Wankathon
         After you graduate
         If you want

OSCAR   Okay?

NELL   But marry me first

         Beat

OSCAR   And why would I want to do that, Nell?

NELL   Hear me out

OSCAR   This is the worst proposal of marriage I have ever
         heard

NELL   There is a method in my madness

OSCAR   Well I can't wait to hear it

NELL   Well I'm not 'hungry for your delicious peen' if
         that's what you're thinking

         Beat

         I get a husband, which gets *my* dad off *my* back
         You get a wife which gets *your* dad off *yours*

         He thinks

OSCAR   Okay, I do see your point
         Deal

NELL   Excellent
         Plus you'd be really helping me out with the
         whole

> *She gestures south*

> Y'know… purity, chastity situation

OSCAR   Can't you just say you broke it horse-riding?

NELL   What?
Like every halfpenny slag in the village? I don't
think so

OSCAR   You're such a snob

NELL   No, I'm special, there's a difference

OSCAR   You are 'special'
On that we can agree

NELL   …'All great men swim'…

OSCAR   Alright

NELL   *Dearie me*

OSCAR   Alright!

NELL   'I've just been… like… reading a lot of Philip
Sidney actually?'
'I just think he's like… sort of amazing?'

OSCAR   It's just a theory
It's just something I'm working on
But I happen to think that swimming and writing
are the same thing

NELL   What *on earth* is that supposed to mean!?

OSCAR   And I want to write so…

NELL   Oh,
Oh so you're going to drown yourself in the
pursuit of a more accomplished prose style?
Is that it?

OSCAR   Not prose, *poetry*

NELL   Because I'm not sure it works like that Oscar
And even if it is, I have to tell you… *that*

>   *What you just did*
>   *That*
>   Wasn't swimming
>   That was drowning

OSCAR   I got carried away

NELL   Yes,
             By the fucking tide

OSCAR   Okay, okay, okay take Hero and Leander…

NELL   Oh for goodness' sake
             No
             Shan't

OSCAR   You might find it interesting
             You might actually learn something, Nell. Imagine
             that?

             Beat

NELL   Go on then, you smug fuck

OSCAR   Okay
             So the story of Hero and Leander is one of the
             greatest love stories in the western canon
             Christopher Marlowe gets his hands on it and
             turns it into, *perhaps*, the greatest epic poem of
             our age

NELL   Right

OSCAR   And all this
             I think
             Is because it's not just a love story, Nell
             It's also a story about swimming
             Leander's heroic swim across the Hellespont and
             towards the woman he loved
             I think, *formally*, that's saying some…

             NELL*'s hand shoots up*

             I'll take a question from the floor…

NELL   The what?

OSCAR   …What?

NELL   He swims across the what?

OSCAR   Where Europe and Asia meet, there is a channel of
          fast-flowing water called the Hellespont
          Treacherous
          Volatile
          Impassable
          But Leander swims it to be with Hero…

          NELL *raises her hand*

          …Go ahead

NELL   Okay and then what?

OSCAR   What?

NELL   And then what?
          She fucks him, does she?

          Beat

OSCAR   …She is so overcome by his bravery, and his
          virility…

NELL   *Right*

OSCAR   That despite having made *a vow of chastity* to the
          goddess Aphrodite…

NELL   *I see*

OSCAR   She does yeah
          She 'gives herself' to him

NELL   I see
          And that's the end is it?

          Beat

OSCAR   *…Yeah*
          It's a tale of heroism
          And virtue

And chivalry
And swimming
And the writing is incredible because it's *all*
connected by the same psychological thread. This
sort of undulating formal energy that comes from
the ways in which the flowing of the poetry
mirrors the flowing of the water and the rhythm of
Leander's heroic progress...

*NELL puts her hand up but doesn't wait to be
called before she puts it down again and speaks*

NELL   And fucking?

Beat

OSCAR   *...Sorry?*

NELL   It's a tale of heroism and virtue and chivalry and
swimming and blah blah blah
...And fucking

Beat

OSCAR   ...I guess it is, yeah

NELL   Right
And he has the energy for that, does he? After all
that swimming?

OSCAR   He does, yeah

NELL   And this Hero
Despite the name
Does she do any swimming?
Any heroic swimming?
Or is it just an awful lot of vow-breaking and
fucking as far as she's concerned?

OSCAR   Right

NELL   Because you know 'nice guys', Oscar?
You know like... 'nice guy' syndrome?

OSCAR   *...Sure*

NELL   Right
        Well
        This Leander
        To be honest?
        Sounds to me
        If I'm honest
        Like a *really nice guy*

OSCAR   *...Okay*

NELL   'Ooooh, oooh I'm a nice guy'
        'Oooh, ooh I swam the Hellespont'
        'Love me'
        'Love me'
        'Why don't you love me?'
        Um I dunno, maybe because you're an
        emotionally manipulative try-hard douchebag who
        just... turns up... at my front door *completely
        naked*, and demands, since you've gone to all this
        effort, that I'd better fucking fuck you then!?
        I mean, what the fuck!?

OSCAR   Right

NELL   Leaving aside the undertones of severe emotional
        coercion for a second, that is just some *desperate*
        shit

OSCAR   Right

        Beat

NELL   Is that what this is all about, is it?
        All this swim-swim-swimming?

OSCAR   Of course not

NELL   Some total hottie is there?
        Creaming her knickers the other side of Poole
        Harbour, waiting for you to paddle across?
        You sad fuck

OSCAR   Sorry, are you jealous?

NELL   Because you could just buy her a drink, Oscar
        Or talk to her

OSCAR   Because I'm sensing a lot of envy?
        And I'm not sure if it's sexual or intellectual

NELL   Maybe it's boys then?

OSCAR   It's not a boy either

NELL   Because that's fine
        From what I recall, a lot of those Greek dudes
        swung both ways

OSCAR   You're twisting my words

NELL   I'm twisting your words?

OSCAR   You are twisting
        My words, yes

NELL   I am *literally* responding to the words you are
        literally saying, Oscar

        Beat

OSCAR   Okay fine
        Forget Hero and Leander

NELL   Yeah, let's

OSCAR   *Yeah*

NELL   Because listen, it's a great analogy
        I'm loving it
        But perhaps it's not quite doing the 'heavy lifting'
        that you were hoping it might
        From an analogical perspective, I mean

        Beat. He cleans the slate

OSCAR   Swimming and writing are the same thing

NELL   Swimming and writing are the same thing
        Go for it

        OSCAR *thinks*

OSCAR   Right so…
Okay
Okay…

OSCAR thinks. This is his big pitch

All you have is the rhythm of your body, okay?
Of your breathing and of your heart
And you don't know, you're not sure, you're in
too deep to know if you're making the slightest
progress, or if the tide is pushing you back
But throughout all of it, Nell
Regardless of all of it
There is always some slow, perceptible suggestion
that you might be moving forward
Now,
That is a description of swimming, Nell
…That is a description of writing, Nell

He is pleased. Beat

NELL   You're quite a self-involved young man aren't you
Oscar?

OSCAR   And you are clearly very bored, Nell

NELL   Is it a low-embarrassment threshold do you think,
or do you simply lack awareness?

OSCAR   Is it a low-information-retention threshold, do
you think, or are you simply terrified that were
you to *actually* attempt to understand what I am
actually saying you might not *actually*
understand it?

NELL   You condescending cunt, I love you so fucking
much

Beat

OSCAR   Then why do you find it so hard to show it, Nell?
Most people around here give me the benefit of
the doubt

NELL   Yeah well that's not love, Oscar. It's deference
            It's a form of privilege

OSCAR   It's respect

NELL   Well if most people around here can afford you
            more respect, then that's probably because most
            people around here haven't seen your sandy little
            dick

OSCAR   That's it

NELL   What is?

OSCAR   You're getting the penis towel on your head

NELL   Don't you dare

            Beat. He moves towards her

            Oscar, if you come near me with your towel I will
            kill you
            I will literally take your life

            *I'm not really sure what happens next, but I guess
            it involves some kind of chase/wrestling match
            where someone ends up pinned to the ground,
            their mouth stuffed with dick-towel? It is light-
            hearted, well-meant and violent. Eventually they
            are sat in silence*

OSCAR   What were you doing back there, anyway?
            Rummaging around in the sand dunes

NELL   I wasn't perving on you, if that's what you're
            suggesting

OSCAR   No
            Not at all
            Just an odd thing to be doing

NELL   I don't owe you an explanation
            This is my beach

OSCAR   *Your beach?*

NELL   Yes
My family own it don't they?
And yours
Between them

OSCAR   Okay, sorry, and you want to lecture me about
privilege?

NELL   I don't see the connection

OSCAR   You don't see the connection?

NELL   I refuse
I refuse to see the connection

OSCAR   And I'm the one apparently lacking in
self-awareness
Interesting

NELL   Listen,
I can come here on my own, okay?
I can be here on my own and be myself
That's rare for me
You don't know what it's like to not be able to do
that

OSCAR   Right

NELL   So don't judge me for refusing to apologise for
what few luxuries I enjoy

OSCAR   Okay, fine

NELL   And, if you must know, I was having a wank

OSCAR   Oh for fuck's sake

NELL   What?
Does that shock you, Oscar?
Are you *threatened* by that?

OSCAR   It's… just… too much information, thank you

NELL   Well where else am I supposed to crack one out!?
Up at the house, with the ladies' maids and the
grooms-of-the-fucking-stool creeping about?

I can't just rub off a quick one you know
To get past the hoop skirt alone I have to stand on
my fucking head
And if anyone *found* me... it doesn't bear thinking
about

OSCAR   Right

NELL   I'm serious
You remember Sally, worked down the old Crow's
Nest Inn in Swanage?
They caught her, on her lunchbreak, having a good
old...

She performs an action

OSCAR   Right?

NELL   Burnt her as a fucking witch, so there's a
cautionary tale

Beat

That reminds me actually, I'd better head back
before they send out a search party

She starts to leave

OSCAR   Bye Nell

NELL   Come up to the house later?
I'll smash out some tunes on the lute for you or
something

She goes to leave

OSCAR   Nell

She stops

I'm sorry for leaving
I'm sorry for leaving you here

NELL   Don't be, Oscar
I'm your number-one fan, you know that
Be bold, don't let me stop you

Three – A Break of Play

Again
It's happened again
Movement
Energy
It's kinetic

If there's a sense of order then it's gone to shit
There is the ghost of a game and there are rules we can't see

Music again
LOUD MUSIC again
The same music AGAIN!
That's annoying
It SHOULD BE annoying
This whole thing is fucking annoying and frankly it's
INCONVENIENT

NELL*! Change into some frothy Regency nonsense*
OSCAR*! Change into your swimsuit*
(*Flannel is it? Fetching*)
Show off your swimsuit, OSCAR. *Show off your muscles!*

Eat snacks, chat shit, have a laugh
But not too much
Remember this song WILL END

Focus now, you need your props – There's no going back if you
forget them
Focus now, remember your lines – There's no going back if you
forget them

Has the music stopped yet? Maybe not? Maybe that's fine?
Remember your lines
Say your lines!
Say them!
Say this!

—   It is 1810... or 1811

—   It is also 1843 *and* 1847

—   Time collapses as it hurtles forward

—   Oscar has graduated and Nell has learned to swim

—   Both are looking forward to one last long summer in this beautiful, but changing place

—   Perhaps the last they will share together

—   Not that they know that for sure

—   Who does?

—   There's melancholy in the air

—   A sense of foreboding

—   A sense that something might be ending

Four – A Scene

Waves lap on the shore, and the seagulls still cry. Sunshine

OSCAR *wears period-specific swimwear and modern reading glasses. He sits reading a ye olde newspaper.* NELL *is stood, in a Regency or early-Victorian dress, playing keep-me-ups with a bat and ball*

NELL	So he does a few lengths Waddles out of the water spouting some nonsense about the 'curative powers of saltwater' And suddenly here we are Suddenly the English seaside is the place to be It's ridiculous
OSCAR	It's not *that* ridiculous
NELL	And all because some mad old git decides to take a dip off Weymouth Pier
OSCAR	*Yes*, but a mad old git who happens to be King George the Third He's an influential man, Nell. It's hardly surprising

Beat. NELL *hits the ball at* OSCAR. *He stops reading*

…Why did you do that?

NELL	You're supposed to be on my side
OSCAR	*I am*
NELL	You don't know what it's been like. You've not been here. This whole place swarming with fat northern daytrippers every Bank Holiday weekend I mean, what even *is* a weekend? Whose stupid idea was that!?

OSCAR   Factory work can be pretty grim, Nell

NELL   Yeah well I miss the good old days. Indentured
         servitude's too good for them

OSCAR   Well they're not here now, so perhaps we could
         just take it down a notch, okay?

NELL   Oscar, this beach is all I have!

OSCAR   I know

NELL   Had!

OSCAR   You need to calm down
         Get out of all that crinoline
         If that is crinoline
         Is that crinoline?

NELL   I don't know. I don't know what crinoline is

OSCAR   Well whatever it is, you must be roasting
         Wriggle on out of it and go for a swim or
         something

         *OSCAR starts reading again. Beat. NELL finds
         more balls and fires them at OSCAR who ignores
         them for as long as he can*[3]

         …Why are you doing that!?

         She speaks as though quoting

NELL   'New regulations state that any lady wishing to
         enter the water'
         'Must'
         'In the interest of modesty and propriety'
         'Descend from the relative obscurity of a bathing
         machine'

         Beat. He thinks

3. In the original production we cut the balls because Alice (the actor playing
Nell) had such despicably bad aim. Instead the choice of projectile changed
daily – carrots, Starbursts and punches were all thrown.

OSCAR   …Oh! The wagon thingies

NELL   The wagon thingies, exactly
          Because although sea-swimming might be replete
          with any number of *mystical curative properties*,
          to catch sight of a stray tit, or a loose pube, in the
          process of having said swim, could apparently do
          any amount of lasting psychological damage

OSCAR   Right

NELL   And since the wagon thingy for Studland Beach is
          owned and operated by a woman called *Linda*
          And since *Linda* is off today because her kid's got
          gout
          Or scurvy
          Or fuckin'… *rickets*
          Or some other perfectly boring, lower-middle-
          class, nutritional deficiency…

OSCAR   Wow

NELL   I can't just 'go for a swim' after all, as it happens,
          Oscar
          And so I am just going to have to sit here and
          quietly fucking bake to death instead

OSCAR   Quietly?

NELL   Yes

OSCAR   You're going to do that quietly?

NELL   Yes!

OSCAR   Right, well let me know when you've started
          because I've read the same three sentences here
          eleven fuckin' times

NELL   Oh you are so lucky I'm out of balls![4]

          *She flops backwards onto the sand in frustration
          and is finally still. She pulls out a book, and puts*

---

4. Again, this line was cut, and replaced with random acts of violence

on a pair of modern tortoiseshell reading glasses.
Silence. OSCAR *has watched her do this,*
eventually he speaks

OSCAR   Well this is fun
It's nice to be back
Nice to see you're keeping so well

NELL   You're a sarcastic little bitch, Oscar. I'm going to
kill you in your sleep

OSCAR   Oh are you?

NELL   Any moment now you're going to put that paper
down and take a long, undergraduate snooze in the
sun

OSCAR   Oh am I?

NELL   You won't be able to resist. The habit's too
ingrained
But once you do
I am going to come over there
And I am going to sit on your smug little face
And I am going to smother you to death with all of
this ludicrous extraneous fabric

OSCAR   Right

NELL   Because there must be some use for it
And I think I might just have discovered what that
is
And it's a *real* shame because I was *really* looking
forward to having you back but you've just gone
and ruined it

Beat. She reads

OSCAR   Have you really missed me *that much*?

NELL   That's no reflection on you, I can assure you
Things have just got distinctly shitter around here
since you've been away, that's all

Pause. She reads her book

OSCAR   What you got there?

NELL   *Jane Eyre*

OSCAR   Any good?

NELL   Not really
Read your newspaper Oscar. I don't want to have
to interact with you for the rest of the afternoon

They both read in silence

OSCAR   Oh my God

Beat

Oh. My. God

NELL   What now?

OSCAR   He's done it
He's actually done it

NELL   Who's done it? Done what?

OSCAR   Fuck

NELL   Oscar!?

OSCAR   Lord Byron
He swam the Hellespont

Beat. She thinks

NELL   Wait, hang on
Pet bear?
Shagged his nanny?
The creepy fucker?

OSCAR   Yeah!
He swam the Hellespont!

NELL   Yeah, okay, I don't care

Beat. OSCAR *reads the article, eventually he
speaks*

OSCAR   This is huge
         This changes everything

NELL   Does it?

OSCAR   Well, I'd put it all to bed, hadn't I?

NELL   Had you?

OSCAR   I'd put it all behind me
         I was going to run that factory Dad's building up
         north
         But now...

         He jumps up

         I'm going to do it
         I'm going to do it too
         By this time next year, Nell, I will have swum the
         Hellespont

NELL   You're an idiot

OSCAR   I'm going for a swim

NELL   Absolutely not! No way!

OSCAR   What!?

NELL   If I have to sit here then so do you

OSCAR   Oh *come on*!

NELL   I'm serious

OSCAR   Nell!

NELL   I can see the exact outline of your scrotum in that
         flannel get-up Oscar, and I will *rip it* from you if
         you attempt to dip even one toe. Read your
         fucking newspaper

         He sits. There is a long, tentative pause

OSCAR   Come with me

         Beat

NELL	What?
OSCAR	Come to Greece Marry me and come with me
NELL	What are you talking about?
OSCAR	If you're my wife then you can come with me

NELL is horrified

NELL	…Oscar, no
OSCAR	Why not? Look at the Shelleys, they go everywhere together
NELL	Yeah, they're also batshit mental, Oscar It's a ridiculous suggestion

Beat

OSCAR	Well you don't have to look quite so horrified I seem to remember this was your idea
NELL	Yeah well things change And anyway I wasn't serious
OSCAR	Well I am I mean it
NELL	I don't care if you mean it, Oscar. I don't know what it means for you to mean it
OSCAR	Well what the fuck is that supposed to mean?
NELL	It means… It means, Oscar, that you 'meant it' when you said you were going to be a Great Poet, That's all you talked about when you were at uni and then suddenly you're out into the real world for all of eleven seconds and you tell me you want to run your dad's factory instead? And now, apparently, you actually don't want to run the factory after all Do you see what I'm getting at here?

OSCAR   Yeah well I never found my... idiom, before

NELL   Your *idiom*?

OSCAR   But this could be what I *need*

NELL   It's an idiom Oscar, you don't have to go looking
           for it, it's not the fucking G spot
           Most people just... have one, okay?
           Or they create one as they go along
           But guess what? It means you've got to put some
           work in!

OSCAR   Okay well that's a little rich coming from you
           Nell, but whatever

NELL   You *really* think Lord Byron is a Great Poet
           because he swam the Hellespont?
           The reason he's great is because he just got on
           with doing the poetry bit!

OSCAR   It's either Greece or it's Yorkshire, Nell, and either
           you can come with me or you're just going to
           have to get used to the fact that I'm not going to
           be around to entertain you for very much longer

NELL   You really think that's what I want?
           You really think that having me by your side,
           As your wife,
           As your *literally* captive audience,
           You *really* think that's a proper use of my time?
           That is not what I had in mind when I suggested
           we should get married, Oscar, and that is *certainly*
           not what I've got in mind now
           It's incredibly offensive for you to go around
           merrily making life-altering propositions like that

           Beat, then quietly

OSCAR   What life?

NELL   Oh I'm sorry!?
           Do we have a question from the floor?

           Beat

OSCAR   Seriously, what life!?
          Maybe, in some way, I'm trying to save you here,
          Nell

NELL   Oscar, really
          There is so much wrong with that statement

OSCAR   Oh but I'm just supposed to swallow the whole
          'tough-love, pull-your-socks-up-Oscar' routine?
          I love you Nell, but you seem to think you're the
          only one here capable of being patronised
          What would you be missing?
          Lounging around, dodging dodgy suitors and
          reading middle-class, middle-brow, middle-of-the-
          road novels?

NELL   That's not fair

OSCAR   Life isn't fair!
          Your life isn't fair
          And so excuse me if I occasionally fantasise about
          ways in which I might be able to help my very
          best friend to live a life that's worthy of her

NELL   Watching you piss *your* life away is not a life
          worthy of me

OSCAR   Well you've been doing a grand job of it so far

          Beat

NELL   Fuck this
          I'm not having this conversation

          She begins to struggle with her dress

OSCAR   What are you doing?

NELL   Swimming

OSCAR   Oh well you've changed your tune haven't you?
          You can't just be a martyr when it suits you, you
          know?
          Joan of Arc would tell you it's a full-time job

NELL   Yeah well Joan of Arc was a career Catholic with
         a vested interest in frying to death, I'm not
         And anyway, sod it, this is my beach

         She wrestles out of more of her clothes and then
         decides she is ready to go in. She walks towards
         the sea, and then comes back

         Oh, and *Jane Eyre* isn't the middle-of-the-fucking-
         road okay? How dare you?
         It's not groundbreaking, I'll admit it
         Nobody is going to swim the *fucking* Hellespont
         over it
         But for the first time in my life I read these pages
         and I see someone like myself written down in
         front of me
         And I know that I am not alone
         And I feel the beginnings of an interior self, the
         likes of which I did not think I was capable of
         And that is fucking meaningful
         Okay?

         Beat

         Okay!?

OSCAR   Yes!
         Fine okay, Jesus!

NELL   This is my beach
         You can just... fucking... shove it!

Five – A Break of Play

This is a game – Why so serious?
This is a game – Can you try to play nice?
This is a game. This is a game – Now if only we could
remember the rules

Music?
Something else?
Please God let it be something else!
…It's probably the same song

OSCAR *get changed*
NELL, *you're halfway there already*
Get out of that dress and into your swimwear – Interwar
specific
Flannel? Not sure
Fetching? Most certainly

NELL, *get wet*
OSCAR, *get props*
Snacks, snacks, snacks come on!

OSCAR
I'm sorry OSCAR
I'm sorry OSCAR… *but this is going to hurt*

OSCAR, *that leg*
Left or right, you choose
That leg isn't getting out of this in one piece
You need to injure your leg, OSCAR[5]
Because this game, whatever this game is, this game involves
conflict

And suddenly, OSCAR *is alone*

5. In the original production, Annabel (the actor playing Oscar) 'shot herself in the foot' with a Nerf gun.

OSCAR   We enter the twentieth century at the space
         between the two great wars
         Where nothing seems to matter and time contracts
         to the space of a single afternoon
         This afternoon in November, to be exact
         For Nell and Oscar the distance travelled from the
         nineteenth century to now has perhaps been less
         than most
         But it has not been insignificant
         Both will feel the space that has unwittingly
         grown between them
         Both will feel a secret sense of loss which they do
         not imagine to be reciprocated
         But perhaps it is
         Perhaps it always, always is

Six – A Scene

The sound of crashing waves grows and grows, filling the space,
filling and filling it, filling the actors, filling the audience

OSCAR *gazes out to sea. He wears a dark suit and a greatcoat,*
a walking stick in his hand. For the duration of this scene he
will affect a limp. NELL *enters in a bright swimsuit. The*
crashing waves subside. They stand, looking at each other

OSCAR   Hello stranger

NELL   Hello

          OSCAR *holds a towel out for her. She takes it and*
          dries herself

          Thank you
          How are you?

OSCAR   Freezing

NELL   Yeah, it's brisk

OSCAR   I've been stood here thinking 'She'll get out soon'
          'She has to get out soon'

NELL   Yeah sorry
          I get really in to it

OSCAR   You're mad

NELL   I'm sure the village must think so

          Pause. Meaning the stick

          What's all this?
          You been in the wars?

OSCAR   Yeah

NELL   Yeah?

OSCAR   Yeah, I mean… Literally

          Beat

NELL   Shit
          Was that totally the wrong thing to say?

OSCAR   It's fine

          *Pause. He rummages around in the pocket of his
          coat. He pulls out a magazine*

          So I found myself, the other day,
          Flicking through the pages of a respected literary
          supplement

NELL   Oh Jesus

OSCAR   I headed straight to the poetry section, as is my
          wont, and whose name should I find?

NELL   Little old me

OSCAR   Little old you
          Congratulations

NELL   Thank you

          Beat

OSCAR   I thought you might…

          *He pulls out a pen, gesturing that she should sign
          it*

NELL   Oh no
          Oscar, stop dicking about

OSCAR   I mean it
          Please?

          Beat. She autographs it

          Thank you

NELL   No worries

          Beat

OSCAR   Why didn't you mention it?

NELL   Sorry?

OSCAR   It's a big deal

NELL   ...*Yes*

OSCAR   So, you should've let me know

NELL   And how was I supposed to do that, exactly?
You don't write, Oscar
And
You don't reply when I write... so?

Beat

OSCAR   Yes alright, that's a fair point

NELL   *Thank you*

OSCAR   I've been busy, I'm sorry
The factory keeps me very busy

NELL   Factory?

OSCAR   I ended up running Dad's factory?
Up in Yorkshire?

NELL   I remember

OSCAR   When I was injured they took me off the front line
The mill had been requisitioned for war work so
I thought I might make myself useful
I ended up running the place and then, after the
war, I just... sort of... stayed

Beat

How's it been here?

NELL   Here?

OSCAR   Yeah
The town, the pub, the old homestead

NELL   Not a clue mate

Beat

OSCAR   Oh,

NELL   Yeah
          I've not been here
          I've not been here for months
          Just got back yesterday, actually. You're lucky to
          have caught me

OSCAR   Right

          Beat

NELL   You thought I'd just been sat here didn't you?

OSCAR   No
          No, not at all

NELL   Twiddling my thumbs?

OSCAR   No

NELL   You did though, didn't you?

OSCAR   No

NELL   'No' means 'yes' though, doesn't it?

OSCAR   I guess it hadn't crossed my mind either way Nell

          She laughs

NELL   No,
          I guess it hadn't

          Beat

          We went to Greece actually, and to Turkey
          Saw the Dardanelles
          Swam the Hellespont
          Well
          No
          Swam *in* the Hellespont

OSCAR   Right

NELL   We had a paddle

OSCAR   Sorry? We?

NELL	Me and Sasha Sasha and I
OSCAR	Sasha?
NELL	The woman I went travelling with, Sasha
OSCAR	Oh

Beat

In what sense?

NELL	I'm sorry?
OSCAR	In what sense? In what sense did you and her go travelling together?
NELL	In every sense you might care to imagine, Oscar

Beat

OSCAR	Right

Beat

NELL	It's stunning The Med The Hellespont I can see why all your poets spent so much time there
OSCAR	Yes
NELL	If you ever get the chance…
OSCAR	I did
NELL	Honestly, if you ever get the chance then you should get yourself over there…
OSCAR	I did Nell I did I was stationed at Gallipoli That was my posting, during the war
NELL	Right

Beat

OSCAR	Didn't get chance to do much *swimming* though
NELL	No

Beat

OSCAR	I'm happy that you're happy Nell
NELL	Thank you
OSCAR	And I'm happy that you're feeling free, or whatever Feeling free and in love or whatever
NELL	I never said I was in love, Oscar
OSCAR	But actually… Sorry To be honest, I could really do without the whole 'Nell Triumphant' act for a change?
NELL	What's that supposed to mean?
OSCAR	You know Nell. You know what I mean, don't pretend you don't The 'Classic Nell' rhetorical rug-pull in which you wittily upbraid me for my casually held misconceptions about the world, Doing your apparent utmost to make me feel like a total *fucking cunt* Whilst all the while making it look as easy and as spontaneous as diving under a wave
NELL	I'm not sure that's fair, Oscar
OSCAR	Oh please Nell, do me a *fucking* solid and *demurely refrain* on this occasion Because I literally cannot think of anything more boring And because I honestly don't think I have any misconceptions left Casually held or otherwise

Beat

> You love swimming, now
> You love travelling, now
> You *loooove* the pussy, now

NELL   *Jesus*

OSCAR   So what?
Find someone who gives a shit, because I'm afraid
that quite a lot of what *I loved*
Quite a lot of what *I* believed in
Has been destroyed
The leg is the least of my worries, but it does
stand as a pretty potent reminder that, as hard as
I might've tried, I could never simply 'go back' to
how things were

NELL   I *never* suggested that you should go backwards
That's you saying that

OSCAR   I'm glad you're writing Nell

NELL   I never said that you weren't

OSCAR   I'm glad you're finding the space and the time and
the freedom to do that now

NELL   I never said that you weren't, Oscar!

OSCAR   But I couldn't, okay?
I couldn't come back here
I couldn't be here and be alone and have *nothing*
and simply hope that '*poetry*' or 'whatever' would
fill the space

NELL   Right
Right, I think I'm getting the gist of this now

OSCAR   Rupert Brooke was at Gallipoli, did you know
that?

NELL   I know who Rupert Brooke is

OSCAR   *Was*
Who he was

        Beat

A brilliant man
A brilliant poet
Or rather
Actually
Sorry
Got my facts wrong for a second there
He was *supposed* to be at Gallipoli
He died on the way
He died under a tree
Not quite in my arms, but as near as damn it
And
You know?
For me? In a way?
I feel like poetry, literature, fucking... art died that day too
Because nothing now
Nothing that we do, or say, or make, can possibly bear the weight of what we did to each other out there

NELL laughs

NELL   Sorry

OSCAR   What's so funny?

NELL   Sorry no... let me get this straight
            You can't do poetry any more
            Because you think that *poetry died*
            Under a tree
            In Turkey?

OSCAR   In a manner of speaking
            Yes

NELL   In a manner of speaking...

            Beat

            I'm too cold for this

            She goes to go off, and then returns

            Give me your coat

OSCAR   Excuse me?

NELL   Give me your coat
          I have something I need to say and I need to be
          warm enough to say it
          Give me your coat, Oscar!

          *He does so. She puts it on, shivers a bit, rubs
          herself and jumps around*

OSCAR   Okay... so

NELL   Just!

          *She gestures at him to wait. She huddles to herself,
          on her haunches, gets up and moves around a bit
          more*

          Okay...
          So...
          You didn't come here today to congratulate me,
          Oscar, okay?
          You came here to defend your mediocrity

          Beat

OSCAR   Jesus Christ

NELL   It's okay
          It's really okay. We get this a lot
          We've been getting 'this' *a lot*?
          This sort of... holier-than-thou, 'I've seen some
          shit over there man', kind of bullshit

          Beat

          Because instead of just going
          'Yeah'
          'War is shit'
          'And'
          'Terrifying'
          And
          'I don't like killing other human beings'
          And

'I certainly don't like doing it in the name of some
specious, abstract objective'
Instead of doing that
You men
You fucking men
Decide to construct an entire gigantic jingoistic
death cult to your own sense of inadequacy

OSCAR   Do you have any idea what you're saying?

NELL   Of which you, the survivors, are the high fuckin'
priests
And so you erect these giant... stone... *erections*
In town squares up and down the country
In the hope that if you memorialise hard enough
And lament long enough
Then eventually it might all start to feel a bit like
'meaning'

Beat

And you can just lay the body of Rupert Brooke...
Can't you?
...You can just... *Lay him*
At the altar of your squandered potential
And feel a whole lot better about yourselves
The arrogance of it, Oscar
The idea that if you destroyed *everything* and if
you all just fell *completely* silent
Then
We'd all just
Sort of
Have to do that too
Because nothing could replace you, could it?
Nothing could replace you lot

Beat

Well consider yourselves replaced

OSCAR   Where was your sacrifice Nell?
When have you ever had to sacrifice anything?

NELL   I never had the chance Oscar

OSCAR   However it went
            Whatever happened
            You were always going to be fine
            Because you're rich enough and isolated enough
            to mean that nothing that happened to anyone out
            there could ever really affect you

NELL   What are you talking about, Oscar!?
            I cared about you!
            I longed to hear from you!

OSCAR   You don't care about me, you don't even know me
            You don't even *see* me

NELL   Well what's that supposed to mean?

OSCAR   It means you've only ever seen me for what I
            supposedly represent
            I'm not a person to you, Nell, I'm a system
            You feel like you've been dealt a shitty hand and
            you look at me like I'm the House fucking
            Croupier, but I'm just another player Nell, just like
            you!

            Beat. He goes to leave

NELL   I'm being published

            He returns

OSCAR   I know!

            He goes to leave

NELL   No
            Not in some shitty little magazine
            A collection
            My first collection

            He has stopped. A ghastly pause

OSCAR   Congratulations

Nothing
Nothing
Nothing

Say the line NELL
Say the line and make it end

NELL   Present day... roughly

Seven – A Break of Play

The music
The action
We know how this goes?
We know how this ends?
We can see the costumes
We can smell the snacks
We can hear the music
And the countdown begins

The countdown begins
It begins
OSCAR... *it begins*
OSCAR*?*

NELL *is getting changed out of her bathing suit into the clothes*
she wore to the theatre today
That's good
OSCAR *gets out of his 1930s-wear as far as his underpants and*
socks
That's good
That's right OSCAR

OSCAR *why have you stopped?*
Why are you just looking at her?
Why are you just looking at the clothes and the people?
Do something OSCAR*!*

Play the fucking game!

Of the following, anything that must happen must happen. If it 'must' it must, but if it merely 'might', or 'may' or 'could' or 'should' then it needn't

The events as described should – if they are going to happen – probably happen in the order as given, but they needn't

Everything is now in flux

NELL *must ask* OSCAR *what he is doing*
OSCAR *must refuse to respond*
NELL *must demand that* OSCAR *hurry up*
OSCAR *must not*
NELL *should become curious*
She might become wary
She might throw him the clothes that he wore to the theatre that day
OSCAR *must continue to do nothing*
Suddenly he might do something
He might shout up to the tech box, and they might turn the music off or change the lights
Or they might not
He might do these things himself
He probably should do them himself if they don't do it for him
He might leave the theatre
She might scream all kinds of abuse at him
She might go after him
She might drag him back, in his pants, by his ear
She might do all this, but then she could just wait
*Because he **must** return for some reason*
That reason might be to collect his clothes
He could take the clothes he wore to the theatre today and throw them into the audience
He could take his sixteenth-century clothes and run out of the theatre with them
He could stay and put them on in front of NELL
NELL *could try and stop him*
Or she could watch in disgust
She should be disgusted by him

OSCAR *must attempt to go back in time*

*He **must** attempt to travel back four hundred years*
NELL *should try to stop him, but she **must** fail*

In order to go back in time OSCAR ***must*** *do the following things:*
- *Get dressed into the clothes of the time with added 'time travel accessories'*[6]
- *Make a potion out of the snacks*
- *Make a portal out of:*
  Snacks
  Costume
  Audience
  Light and sound
- *Do a Dance of Remembrance and of Conveyance to a Hype Song of his Choice*[7]

He might share with NELL *what he is doing*

*He **must** make the following argument by way of justification:*

OSCAR   I know how this works Nell
          Okay?
          We stand on the beach and we talk and I say
          something wrong
          I always say something wrong because the fucking
          goalposts of what is and isn't appropriate keep
          moving
          All the time
          And I sort of finally and painfully come to
          understand what you're saying
          And then they play the music and we get changed
          And
          Suddenly
          Bang!
          Suddenly we're somewhere new, again
          And I simply do not understand, again
          And
          I'm done
          I'm done with it

6. In the original production this meant a variety of things depending on Annabel's (the actor playing Oscar) mood – goggles, a hard hat, a life jacket, flippers, a big pink furry jacket, etc.
7. Regular favourites included Cher, the *Downton Abbey* theme and the theme from *Planet Earth*.

And
I am going back to the last time that the version of
myself that I have in my head somehow matched
my sense of the world into which I was placed
And you know what?
I think that's pretty fucking reasonable

She could tell him that it isn't reasonable

She could sympathise

*She might try to stop him at any time and by any
means she deems necessary*

**But he must attempt to go back
He must attempt his Dance of Remembrance and
of Conveyance**

NELL **must** *interrupt the dance
She might bring the house lights up
She should probably cut the music
She should persuade him that he has failed... it
will probably be obvious that he has*

NELL **must** *then make the following speech*

NELL   I had some swimming lessons once
            A while back
            Because nobody had ever bothered to teach me
            Nobody had thought that I could, or should
            And
            As part of the course they taught us some basic
            life-saving skills
            They warned us that if a person is drowning
            And
            You approach them
            Then the fear and the panic they feel might induce
            them, against all reason or logic,
            It might induce them to push you under the water
            So that they can stay above the swell

            Beat

I sort of feel like that is what you're doing, Oscar
You're pushing me down instead of letting me
take you
Instead of letting me take hold of you, and bring
you back to shore
You're going to drown
And before you drown
You're going to drown me
And I can't let you do that Oscar
I can't

Beat

This
This is me breaking your grip
Okay?

Beat

Because what is the plan here, Oscar?
Do I come back with you?
Do you do your little dance and then we all, all of
us here
We all go back with you into Oscar-land?

Beat

Because you can't want that for me mate
You can't

Beat

We don't get to choose
We move forward
The world we live in changes
Sometimes for the better, but not exclusively
Sometimes it gets worse
And we have to have the confidence
And the grace
And the fortitude
To move with it
And to find our place within it
And that's it

He should be vulnerable
She should be kind
*She **must** persuade him to make an attempt at the*
final scene
He might get dressed into the clothes he wore to
the theatre, or his sixteenth-century clothes or his
pants
He might be able to negotiate a deal whereby he
does the scene but only if he gets to wear the ruff
or tights
*To a greater or lesser extent both **must** accept*
responsibility for what follows and what has so far
come to pass

Sometimes the actors act the following

Sometimes they simply say it

Sometimes they are not at all interested in what
they are saying

Sometimes they have visibly lost all confidence in
the world of the play

Sometimes they have lost all confidence in the
playwright and the playwright's craven desire for
easy resolutions

Sometimes they are keen to identify and stress
strongly the ways in which the playwright has
cleverly problematised the resolution of his play

Sometimes they have no patience for subtlety

Sometimes it feels quite sore

The rules are broken. The play is ending. The
world is dying

NELL *and* OSCAR *sit in the space in silence*

Eventually they do the scene

NELL   It's warm today

            Silence

OSCAR   I think I might do an MA

NELL   Yeah?

OSCAR   Yeah
            Might do an MA, might do a PGCE
            Not sure

            Beat

NELL   Do the MA

OSCAR   Yeah?

NELL   Do something for yourself Oscar

            Beat

OSCAR   Yeah

            Silence

NELL   *'The Hellespont – Classical Allusion and its Place*
            in Masculine Literary Culture'
            Something like that

OSCAR   It's been done

NELL   Not by you

            Beat

OSCAR   Yeah okay, I'll do that
            Get the doctorate
            Teach the module
            Pick out the prettiest girl in the class and marry
            her

NELL   Oh for goodness' sake

OSCAR   I'm joking, Nell

NELL   I know
         I know you are

         Beat

OSCAR   But I would like that
         A teammate would be nice

NELL   Yeah
         I guess you're right

         Beat

OSCAR   What about you?

NELL   Haven't the time mate

         He scoffs

         I haven't!

OSCAR   I bet if you added up all the hours that you've sat
         on this beach with me you'd've had the time

NELL   Poetry isn't what it was you know
         You can't just knock it out any more
         People actually expect you to go to places and
         read it out to them
         Aloud
         Festival after festival
         Spoken fuckin' Word nights

         Beat

         Actually that reminds me, I'd better be going
         Question Time's in Bournemouth tonight
         They've had someone pull out so I'm going on

OSCAR   I didn't know current affairs were your thing

NELL   My agent said I should do it
         Said that, if it all goes well, I could get myself a
         column in the *New Statesman* or something

OSCAR   What would you write about?

         She shrugs

NELL   They'd want the bog-standard liberal identerist
          bullshit I guess

OSCAR   D'you think?

NELL   All I know is that people don't tend to look at me
          and think 'hmm I wonder what she thinks about
          Israel'?

          Beat

          Anyway
          Tune in
          Let me know what you think

OSCAR   Sure

          She doesn't go to leave. Beat

NELL   Oscar…

OSCAR   Yeah

NELL   Don't get mad

          Beat

OSCAR   *Okay?*

          Beat

NELL   Oscar… Do you really want to be an academic?

OSCAR   Ah

NELL   Isn't there something else that you want more than
          that?

OSCAR   Nell…

NELL   Because it was your dream wasn't it?
          And
          I know that by some fluke of chance I've ended up
          doing it
          But that doesn't
          Like
          Void your dream

OSCAR   No

NELL   It doesn't make it ridiculous

OSCAR   I never said it did

Beat

NELL   No
No I guess you didn't

He shrugs

OSCAR   I don't know, Nell
All I know is that the world doesn't work like that
All I know is that I liked university
I felt good there
I felt like I belonged

NELL   You can't go backwards Oscar

OSCAR   No
But I can return

End of Play

A Nick Hern Book

Wild Swimming first published in Great Britain in 2019 as a paperback original by Nick Hern Books Limited, The Glasshouse, 49a Goldhawk Road, London W12 8QP, in association with FullRogue

Wild Swimming copyright © 2019 Marek Horn

Marek Horn has asserted his moral right to be identified as the author of this work

Front cover photography: Alice Lamb as Nell by Chelsey Cliff
Back cover photography: Annabel Baldwin as Oscar by Chelsey Cliff

Designed and typeset by Nick Hern Books, London
Printed in Great Britain by Mimeo Ltd, Huntingdon, Cambridgeshire PE29 6XX

A CIP catalogue record for this book is available from the British Library

ISBN   978 1 84842 912 3

CAUTION   All rights whatsoever in this play is strictly reserved. Requests to reproduce the text in whole or in part should be addressed to the publisher.

Amateur Performing Rights   Applications for performance, including readings and excerpts, by amateurs in the English language throughout the world should be addressed to the Performing Rights Manager, Nick Hern Books, The Glasshouse, 49a Goldhawk Road, London W12 8QP, *tel* +44 (0)20 8749 4953, *email* rights@nickhernbooks.co.uk, except as follows:

New Zealand: Play Bureau, PO Box 9013, St Clair, Dunedin 9047, *tel* (3) 455 9959, *email* info@playbureau.com

Professional Performing Rights   Applications for performance by professionals in any medium and in any language throughout the world should be addressed in the first instance to Nick Hern Books (address above).

No performance of any kind may be given unless a licence has been obtained. Applications should be made before rehearsals begin. Publication of this play does not necessarily indicate its availability for amateur performance.